50 Poems, 100 Moons

Edward Valladao

Cover Art & Illustrations by
Mia Ohki

D0444432

Words and Cover Art Copyright © 2018
Edward Valladao

Illustrations Copyright © 2018 Mia Ohki

All rights reserved.

for

beginners

at

love

I.

Heaven forgive him
who has the choice of two
burning suns;
Whether to luxuriate safely
in the warmth of one
or to be destroyed by a
Heat of passion
before the
other is gone.

2

II.

Mid-morning
tip-toe
with your bathrobe
half-open

Sun rays
steal glances
at your nacreous
body
through closed blinds

chin held high,
lithe legs glide,
a sly smirk
gives us both away

Mid-morning
awe
with one eye
half-open

My and the Sun's
favorite time of day

4

III.

How fitting
it was that you lined
your walls with Christmas lights
Every time I set foot
into that room
could you not
see the wonder in my eyes?

The swing of the blue door
and the rush of love I felt
at the very sight of you,
how it dissolved all those
insignificant things that broke me
throughout the week

Nothing ever remained
but the soft eerie
glow
reflecting off your face,
you sitting there enchanted
on the bed
nothing but
a coy look
and a smile
behind a book

Passing out of
one world
and into another.

IV.

Don't eat, she said,
I'm cooking dinner.

All week he could not hide his curiosity
not only because she had made it clear
from the get go she was
NOT
that type of woman,
the type to slave over a stove
for
SOME
man.

No,
his curiosity burned over the
fact that she did not even own a stove!
There in that small apartment whose
privacy she cherished so much.

He drove an hour,
his weekly ritual,
only to get a surprising admonishment.

You're early! Why are you so damn early?!

She throws a sweaty wisp of hair off
her gleaming forehead
and disappears,
running back inside to her preparations,
a small hot plate

on a chair.

Her eyes water.
I'm sorry, she says,
crestfallen.
It's taken hours
and
I've only made three.

He looks past her to the only
furniture in the room,
a small coffee table,
barren
except for
one plate
with two pancakes,
the third currently
in the slow simmering works.

For a second, he forgets that
he is starving
and
lets out a mad laugh as
he embraces her.

His eyes water
and she's hurt.

That goddamn hot plate,
she says,
I remember you said
you like pancakes
and...

and…
Why?
Why are you so damn early all the time?

But in this moment
she misconstrues
his smile,
his tears,
his laughter,
unaware of
how tragically late,
how embarrassed
he now feels

to feel loved
for the first time
in this way.

V.

Years earlier I had
done away with
church, praying,
God and the bible,
the whole deal
because none of it ever
seemed to hold up its
end of the bargain.
I didn't curse the skies,
I simply paid religion
no more mind,
left it locked away
in the halls of my past
and went about my life.

Until your laughter let
it out again,
Mocking laughter
that erupted at the
foolishness of every sacred
sight.
My god, I thought,
What happened to this woman
to make her curse the heavens
so brazenly?
I didn't dare say that
out loud
nor did I tell you
how there was something
Divine

in that laughter,
your absolute madness
of spirit,
that was starting to make
me a believer
all over again.

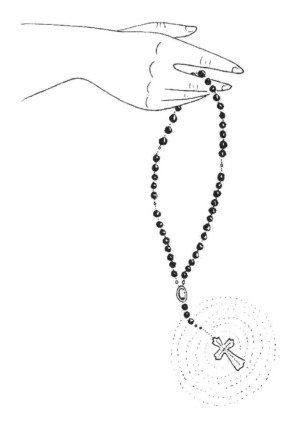

VI.

your cracks
show
and sometimes the glue will
not hold
for your sake
I will pretend
my eyes do not
see what others
have done
and when you break me
I will not be able to
pretend that parts
of me are not
lost forever
even then
in the hopeless end
I will remain blind
always
for your sake

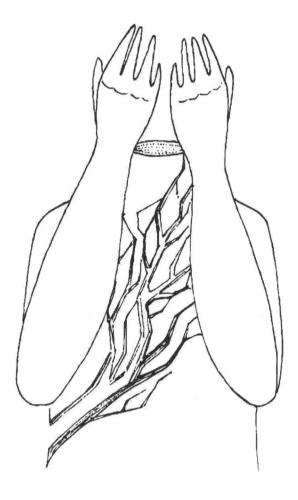

VII.

Her brows flicked and danced
to mask the weight of fallen kingdoms,
unaware that I, too, carried them
with every stolen glance.

Her legs, smooth as alabaster,
more precious than priceless pearls,
belied a never-ending exodus
felt only in sleep with every subtle scrape
against my own.

Her eyes, dark as the darkest depths,
never to be penetrated,
told a wordless story
only to be understood after their departure.

That there is wildness in this world
that cannot be tamed.
Strength that will never subside.
When it is found in a woman
you cannot contain her,
you must not try.

You cannot quell her mettle
or confine her strengths
to the weaknesses of your own mind.
All you can do is sing her praise
and pray you have what it takes
to match her stride.

VIII.

I watch you,
a beauty too wild for this world,
as if you sprang forth
not from human loins,
but alone,
amongst the trees in an ethereal wood.

I listen to you,
ancient nomad whose history
is held close to her chest.
Spill your secrets,
I will not question your beginnings
nor your goings to and from here,
not today, nor evermore.

I love you
simply,
simply because I know no other way.
I have abandoned reason
and comfort to follow you.
Even if you should lead me
to the depths of suffering
in a foreign land,
I will trust you
for it is your love
and only your love
that will
lead me out.

IX.

My Love,
do not slide back into
that cavern of loneliness
wherever you are.
Your stay has expired,
my hands have sealed it shut.
If false circumstances
feign love
and foster pain,
do not be swallowed
in a sea of anger,
my heart has already
drank it for you.
And if you cry,
know your cries
do not slip away
into the darkness
of an open sky.
I pull them into me
like the tides,
a Moon made to
hold onto your light
while you sleep.

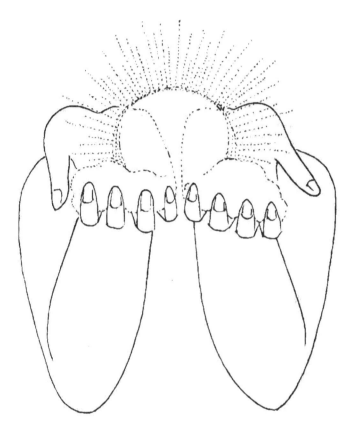

X.

Separate fragments
connect,
their wholeness
felt but not seen

The nape of a neck
nestled into a chest.
A smile.
Two dancing heartbeats.
Four closed eyes.

XI.

To dance with no music
while the roots of my
past left me shackled.

To sing your soul's desire
while fear nipped at the toes
of my own to stay silent.

To challenge the world's offerings
while obedience in ignorance
filled my plate.

Two lovers at dinner.
More than space in between.

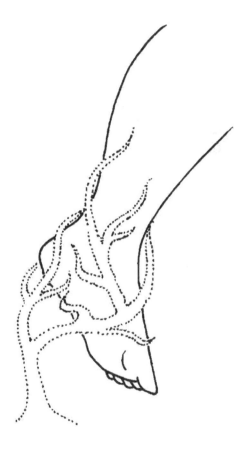

XII.

Vespertine lily,
Conqueress of light,
You drink from
your Wounds
and burn from your Spite.

XIII.

Show me a road map to your heart's desire.
Some nights your love for me is lost
beneath a saltine sky,
a treasure that hides itself
away again once found.
The currents that hold
your affections close
let them drift away without warning.
I feel them pull away even in my sleep.
Dreams of the loss of you
stir me awake to the sight of your back,
my hand placed softly on your hip
causes you to inch away.
Speak to me before morning comes,
before the hills
have stolen your body
along with your love.

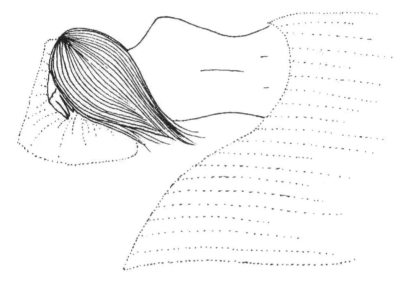

28

XIV.

We peel back each other's
skin with verbal nails.
There's sharpness not
only in your words
but your movements

Ah your movements!

An arm thrashes down
to your side,
half-spin with
a whip of the neck,
your eyes so large,
so dark,
blazing beacons
below a frazzled mane

They signal there will be no escape,
Not on this night

Awash with intensity,
the tides move up to my neck.
Do I fear a cold crescendo?
Or have I just become a voyeur
of your raging beauty?

Am I here
or somewhere else?

XV.

We grew too close,
limbs became entangled,
buds would no longer bloom.
Our tops became crazy,
the heat unbearable,
one would need to be removed.

The axe swung close,
limbs became mangled,
only one left could bear fruit.
I've let myself be cut into pieces,
those pieces
that burn for you.

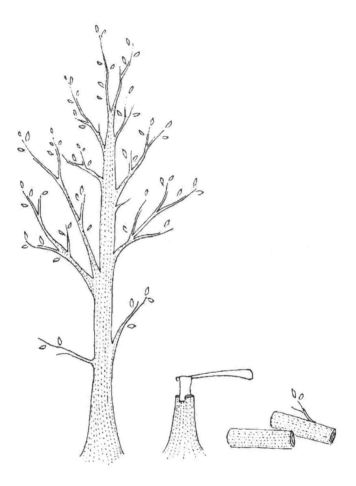

XVI.

I crave love that tears me up out by the root,
throws me into chaos with 100mph winds,
leaves me sucked dry and cracked,
starving and mad
in the valleys of my regrets,
my bones hollow,
broken,
deserted.
Love like Armageddon,
its arrival announced with trumpets
and destruction.
When it comes there will be
no rebuilding,
no need for renewed peace.
Harvest gone and spring an afterthought.
Sowing fire with fire
that burns for eternity.

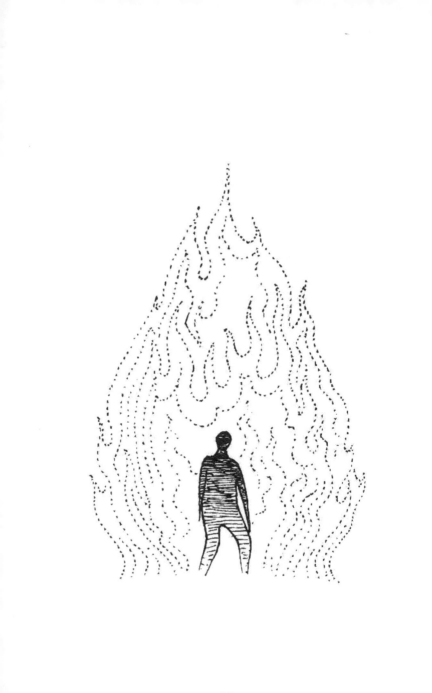

XVII.

harvest came early
but back then we never
picked with the seasons.
so I watched intently
as you broke through the skin,
scooped out my flesh with half-moon hands
and
culled with listless lips
only to spit out the bitterness of my fruits
and the seeds of my stubbornness
as if they were poison.
because they were.
and I watched myself sink
into the darkness of the unforgiving ground,
the barren rinds of my former self
always looming overhead,
sustained in a rainless plain
by the lingering memory of your
sweet saliva.
only to grow
and grow,
to re-emerge in the sun
and find you

Gone.

XVIII.

How strong you could be
I've seen men quiver in your presence
Couldn't you tell I was one of them?
Eventually I saw the strength it took for you to
leave
At the time I hadn't acquired that sort of
strength myself

Though the thoughts entered and left
the port of my mind,
deep down I knew I could never sail
away without you.
Even if you sabotaged my ship
to the bottom of the sea
I would have to learn to breath
underwater
if that's where you wanted to be.

But did you really think your weakness could
not escape?
That you could be so strong and yet still be
drowning
in love for another man
that whole time?
That the remnants of what destroyed you
wouldn't seep into this boat of ours
because you could not let them go?
Don't you know I saw how you hid your hands
from the start?
And still I stayed constant

up until you cast me off
to drown myself.

The irony being that you could never
be with someone
so weak,
someone who reminded you
so much of
yourself.

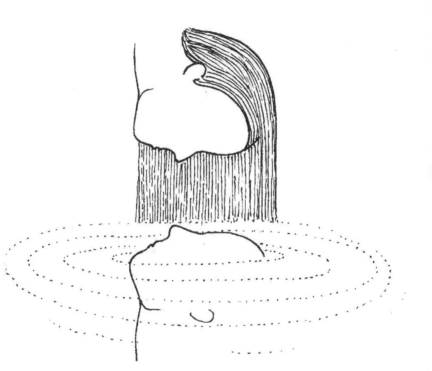

XIX.

For those who bemoan
the elusiveness of the forbidden fruit,
swallow your lamentations
eat your cries,
enjoy the beauty of a garden of ignorance
that gives you life.
For those you call lucky
never get their fill.

Some only get to
taste the skin
while others gorge
on a juiciness
never to be known by their lips again.

The knowledge of pleasure
will seek out your ears,
The taste of happiness
strolls in search of your hunger.

Just remember my naïve neighbors,
my fortunate friends,
the forbidden fruit,
Not you,
decides its end

and when it's gone

that is when the pain
you've never known begins.

XX.

Your name spills onto
my tongue
on sweltering days
but I won't drink.

Your shadows pirouette
to demure symphonies
along walls dimly lit,
in a room
I no longer keep company.

Your voice laves
my soul in sleep

Hypnotizing siren
lure this
willing victim
until cruel morning saves.

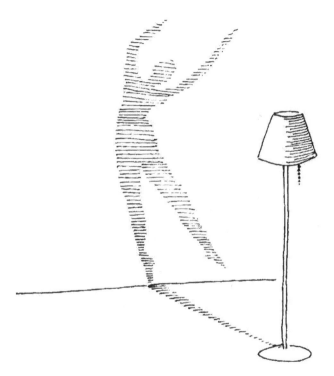

XXI.

Right or wrong,
a debate soon often forgotten.

Claws dull, sinking into new flesh
or silently down to an ocean bottom.

XXII.

all we want is another human
vase
to pour some of our
suffering into

we do it with such pleasure
perhaps that fills us too

and when
the time is up
we get carried away
fearing
more broken pieces to
carry
more suffering

by now
I should know better
I think
you know better than to give
away too much

but you
you will meet
another lover
to pour yourself into
the trouble I've caused you
if not already
then today
this week

surely this month

you will be okay

do not think of me
while I overflow
there is space for me
in this lonely old room
where I try not
to think of you

XXIII.

I traded the Sun
for one hundred moons,
one hundred nights without you.
Do you hear my
screams at the crease?
Do you cringe at the sight
of a flowerbed overrun
with nocturnal weeds
fed on a careless fervor?
Can you sympathize?
or has the Sun never
lacked
Warmth
Light
Love?
Will the Sun always burn in secret,
far away from those foolish
enough to forsake her first?

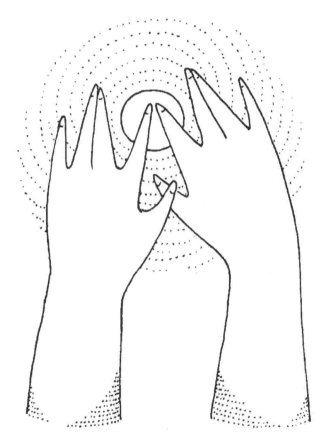

48

XXIV.

A heart ensnared
left for others
to salvage

Love-savaged,
left in smother,
unable to care

Life in guilty acquiescence
or
death in noble desertion?

Accept a savior's arrival
or
hope for a tormentor's return?

XXV.

When you left that small room,
what did you leave behind?

Did you stow away my letters
like secrets
between your fine china?

Or did you abandon them
in the company of several old screws?
Unopened on a dusty old shelf for
the amusement of strangers.

Did you leave every last trace of me in that
small room?

Or was my love obstinate
as I once was,
sliding out of danger
from your determined view,
packing itself away inside
a lampshade,
a deck of cards,
a page in a book.

Do you curse its intrusions
as impolite afterthoughts
or do you silently savor
the succor of its sweet aftertaste?

XXVI.

That day you appeared miraculously
on a sidewalk,
I swerved my car and parked.

Not a word from you in
months and there you were,
a sign,
synchronicity orchestrated
by sympathetic gods.

I could not betray my own suffering
so I ran and found you sitting in a bar
with two strange men,
their ugly faces
scowled at me when yours lit up
at my presence.

I was an invader to these men,
men who only had dreams of
conquering,
too ignorant to know
that the object of their pursuit
could not be conquered,
but alas
one cannot see past's plundered hearts
in that heavenly face.
How I missed that face.

And those arms!

We hugged outside for several seconds.
We both looked good we said
and I knew in the way you looked at me,
perhaps you seen it in me too,

That it was still there,
that unexplainable adhesive
that pulls two strangers together.

You mention that I'm leaving town soon
and, by your comment, I know
you've read my letters.
I do not ask why you have not replied.
Instead, I smile sadly and cut our reunion short,
the resulting sadness in your face
giving me an illusive sense of power
that meant nothing.

We must meet again before you leave,
you said.
I agreed, and we hugged again
for several seconds.

As you headed back inside, I watched
your backside
and then those two ugly men who skulked
behind the window
like buzzards,
their faces morphing
into feigned delight to match yours
as you slid in front of them.

I rushed to the train station

trying not to look at the time,
knowing good well I was already
twenty minutes late
before your unexpected intrusion
on my feebly rebuilt peace.

I could never keep time in your presence
but oh how time became magnified
in your absence.

God I was late!

When I swerved into the station parking lot
she sat alone
under the sadness of a street lamp
and an overcast sky,
the South American girl whose name
I have forgotten,
one of a handful
I had entertained in a fruitless effort
to pry you from my mind.

She was due to leave the country in a few days,
had taken the train several hours to
spend her last weekend with me.
I had agreed to this tryst
as a personal test to get over a love that
would not listen.
How could I have known that the universe
had been watching, listening all along?

She cried as I explained the truthful
reason behind my lateness,

the same reason why she must get back
on the train immediately and go back home
wherever that was.
She would not accept my money for the fare
or my apologies.
She cried
silently,
out of sorrow, anger,
or both,
I do not know.

And as I drove home
alone
I finally knew what it felt like
to feel terribly righteous
and righteously terrible
all at once, both in the past
and present.
I marveled at fate's strange lessons
and rejoiced in my rare moral victory,
clearly earning a new future,
clearly deserving of a second chance
with you, the one I truly loved.

If you're wondering why I never
told you that story
or how I felt that day
it's because I feared you'd never
see me again

and you haven't

so what do I have left to fear?

XXVII.

When all around me slumbers
and the sunset sighs
the shades of tomorrow,
the impossibility
of a life re-lived
blows a torpid breeze.
The stars, the moon have lost their luster,
a darkness swallows the sea.
I struggle to carry
the weight of sorrow
on silent nights like these.

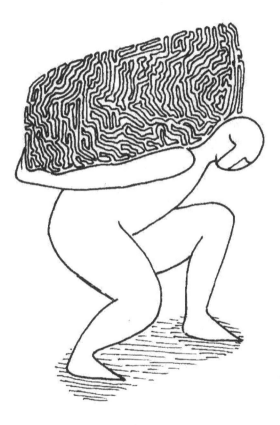

XXVIII.

For months,
after the cataclysmic crash left
a crater never to be re-filled,
a hellish haze hung over
my eyes and my heart.
In the chaos, I could not see myself
nor who I once was.
I reached out blindly,
careless arms latching onto
any semblance of your stability
but foreign fingers only
picked at my conscience,
pushing me further into
the dark hole of my own creation.

How could I be angry that you escaped?

In that lonely darkness I prayed in silence
for your safety, your happiness,
your forgiveness,
Not my freedom,
Not light, nor sound.

In my own destruction,
a glimpse of a world of beauty lost
and a love that could fill
at long last found.

XXIX.

we had to teach ourselves,
how else would we learn?
There were no classes,
no formal training on such a precarious subject.
they taught us about the world,
everything necessary to make a living.
But to obtain that which makes us feel alive…

well, for that, we've always been on our own.

so we studied like children,
mimicking the ways of the other,
looking for answers
that neither one of us had,
nevertheless unwilling
to admit
such a common flaw.

soon, in inexperienced hands,
our knowledge became weapons,
perceived lies could be only be assuaged
by real ones.
suspicions begat suspicions
regardless of the truth.

up until the end,
the more guarded we both became.
and when you left, the only thing
left to study were all my past mistakes.

the less we know about love
the more we learn to hurt.
the more we're hurt
the more we learn to love.
the more we know about love.
the less we hurt.

thank you for teaching me
when no one else could
and if I could not reciprocate
please forgive me for my childish ways

XXX.

your pain spilled
out in teaspoons
measured always
yet I drank
hid it deep
in an unknown place
severed from the source
yet still growing by
the day
knowing now
it was all carried
in vain
for every teaspoon
consumed
was foolishly twice
replaced.

XXXI.

Send a decree to the trenches
of a turbulent sea
and I will drown in love to meet you there.

Or if befits,
command a covenant
on the highest mount.
Safety cannot tempt my restless climb.

I am the great deceiver,
who else but I knows how far
the fall from paradise?

I do not fear the ills
of this world my love,
rather my eternal torture
lies in the absence of heaven's ear,
the absence of absolution,
a reservoir to pour my spoiled pride.

I roam this prison,
waiting for your mercy to save me
from what I hold inside.

XXXII.

I've called upon the forces for your return,
daily supplications unheard.
Stranded in a home re-built
from the rubble,
I study its walls, their material,
contemplating their strength
in times of love impetuous.
Will it even matter?
Have the trade winds pulled you away
and sank to the ends
of a world too large to contemplate?
Did you find walls strong enough to hold your
love?
Or did it seep out through the cracks
like my insecurities,
left in a time and place not worth re-visiting.
Would I make the same mistakes,
stuck in my ways?
or would I traverse your body
like the streets of an unknown city,
cautious and with wonder.
Would I listen to every word from your lips
with fullness and understanding
like an ancient knowledge
lost at birth?
or would my own stay dormant,
haunting me,
metamorphosing,
forever in fear of the absence of yours.

Shall I wait on the forces who say, "Patience,
patience, please!
Men more deserving now call upon me.
You've had your chance.
Now be quiet, please!"
Or shall I instead line these paper walls
which, like your love, have given me
the strength to rebuild,
for others to study,
to not make the same mistakes
to be able to finally,
unequivocally say,
I love you.

XXXIII.

No more time for abbreviation
or footnotes.
Though my hand aches
from writing the story of my heart
I will not put my pen down
nor hide my antagonists
in allusions cloaked in surly syntax,
for only history can reveal
the true protagonists.
So let the oil burn and
the ink drain.
I will lose sleep pondering
past loves' sleepless nights
during the paragraph
breaks of my life.
Each of us has been
punctuated by pain,
but while others format,
edit, and erase,
I promise not to let one iota
escape
and in doing so
do the hardest thing.

Change.

XXXIV.

I used to only feel loved
with plainspeak.
Yet lovers whose words
flowed like rapids
were caught and driven quickly
away themselves.
And though briefly cooled, I, in turn,
was slow to believe them.
Even so, I desired from you
that which would not easily come,
the longer restrained,
the more agony and pain.
And when those words
scuttled out at long last
in a whisper,
quick was I to question my own deafness.
Too fixated to feel
to see
that the language of
your hands,
your lips, your eyes,
your body
all along
spoke plainly
and spoke only to me.

XXXV.

Oh how the months roll away,
fingertips cold, slowly
forgetting the feel of May.
The power of one word
kept at bay
and a thousand poems
written
just to remember your face.
Oh how the years roll away.

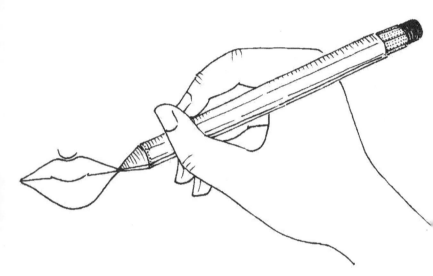

XXXVI.

We mistook each other for sanctuary,
two shipwrecked travelers
pulled together by separate storms.
Turned fortune into fate,
turned rough weather into
a sweet sojourn.

But calm waters made
our minds drift in secret
back onto their course.

Your soul's sail blew east,
mine pulled back to the west.
We turned fate back into fortune,
corrected our compasses
towards true north.

Now miles gained equals miles lost.
We race in opposite directions
for what we had at the start.

XXXVII.

my heart
play this part
perform your never-ending soliloquy
though at times
you tire of lonely lines
though at times
you crave the adulation
of an audience
that may or may not
be there
do you dare?
do you dare break
the fourth wall
at your own discretion?
or must you sit here?
sit here
and wait for outside direction?
my heart how long?
how long
must
my heart
play this part

XXXVIII.

in the ashes
I have become dust.

I can wait an eternity
for the hands of an ocean
to pull me under
to mold me into a new creation

or I can wait

wait for the clashing
I hear
below the surface
to cease.

to sink into a fault
never to be seen or felt

or to rise

to grow high
with time
into a mountaintop.

in the ashes
I have become dust.
all dust can do is
wait to change.

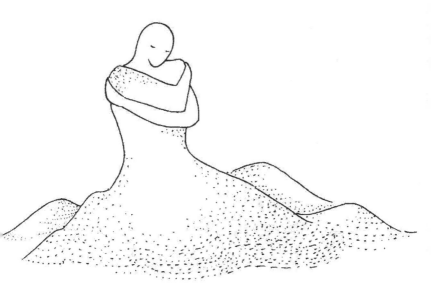

XXXIX.

We all have it.
Every single one of us.
It reeks from our bones,
screaming, clawing,
desperate to clamor
out through the membranes
of our entire being.
To make us whole
like the time before we were born.

Love unborn.

If only we felt we
deserved the love
we were born to give,
maybe then we would
know how to truly live.

XL.

There are no last straws
in love.
You can carry its weight
or you can look
to replace with
a lighter load.

If you've started
counting straws,
please be courteous,
count them loud
so that I may know
there no longer is
love left in you
for me
to count on.

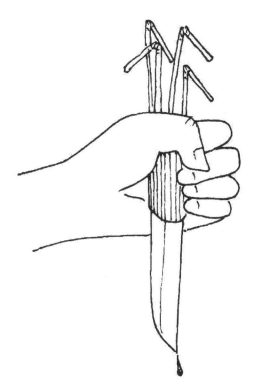

XLI.

How to find love:
Don't try. It can only find you.

How you will know love is there:
You will change.

How to hold onto love:
Give it back without reservations.

How to cope when love is taken away:
Find yourself.

How to find yourself:
Be patient while you wait for love to find you
again.

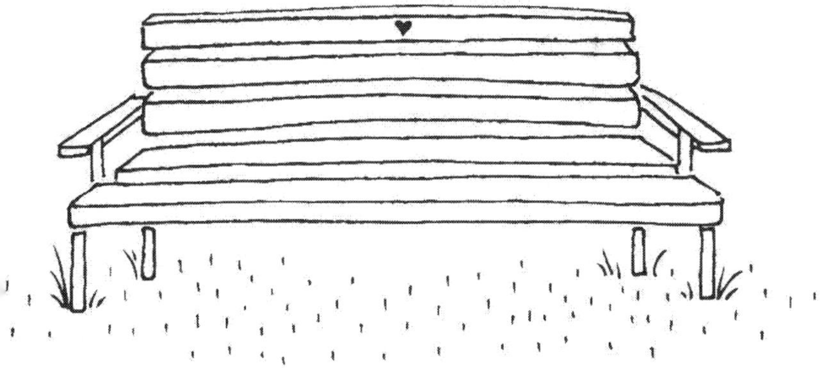

XLII.

we're either making
mistakes
or waiting for strangers
to make mistakes
somewhere
on nights
where dishes break
and the coyotes
howl
the snake oil salesmen
of the world
are found out
and the lonely
men and women
of the world
can't hear anything
but the
thum thum
drip drip
of their own
melancholy
collecting at their feet

XLIII.

Thoughts of the end
will only consume,
Don't you know
the end has no concern for you?
It wanders,
lonesomely searching out uncertainty
to fill its bellicose belly.

Do not let its visions strangle away
your heart's hold on the pleasures
of the present.
To do so will only
hasten its eager and destructive arrival.

Live and love so fully
in this world
that Death will have no choice
but to pass you on to another,
the radiance of your soul so bright,
it burns a hole right through
Death's cold clutch.

Live like this
and
you will become
a star that blooms
in future's darkest hours,
a lucent reminder that
fearless love lives on
even after we're gone.

XLIV.

On my worst days
your name slips off
my tongue like a healing mantra,
a sacred balm to sooth the truth.

On my best days,
when all is calm,
its charms are of no use.
Back then I called you mine my love,
those days I spent with you.

XLV.

there is strength gained from living apart
the blade cuts
bullets penetrate
but a love lost is a latent beast
it tears and churns
your insides
slowly
pangs strike without notice
from a world
unknowing
yet complicit
there is no remedy
there is no cure
a weakness only becomes
strength
the more pain,
the more years endured

XLVI.

We are
two rivers running
parallel
from a common
basin,
Should land divide
us along our path,
it is but a
brief
illusion on the surface,
For you are in me
and I in you,
We are both
one and
separate,
forever flowing back towards
one another,
held invisibly
together
by our beginning
and the end.

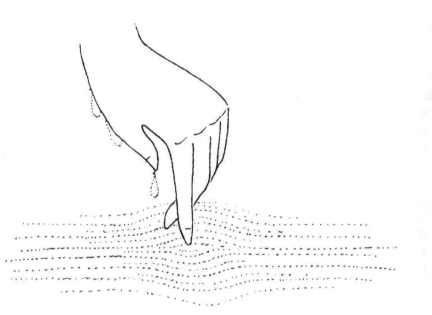

XLVII.

twenty-eight years old
and I haven't touched
a woman in over a year.
not a kiss
not a hand held,
nothing but old
memories to hold onto
beneath the same old sun.
on most days the warmth
of invisible rays
is enough.
on others
I don't feel a thing.

XLVIII.

Temperance has always been
my biggest battle.
I've never been
able to quite conquer
it.

Either I'm boiling over,
sick with love
or
I retreat back
into hibernation
alone
with dreams
of a never-ending winter.

Is my failing battle
the result of adverse
conditions?
or are they simply
the conditions of
a particular heart?

XLIX.

took a few years
but I'm doing better now.
I no longer have to wince
at my reflection
or ruminate over
senseless acts
of the past.
not as much at least.

still broke despite
what I promised.
come to find my
heart wants very little
in this life.
I've found I'm happier this way.

not to mention
I can't say I'm in
bad company now.
I've grown on myself
after all these lonely nights together.

every now and then
when the moon
sneaks through
I must admit
I wonder about you

how much you
must have changed

after all these years,
how everything changes
whether we like it or not

and that's when I catch myself,
remembering…

some things never do.

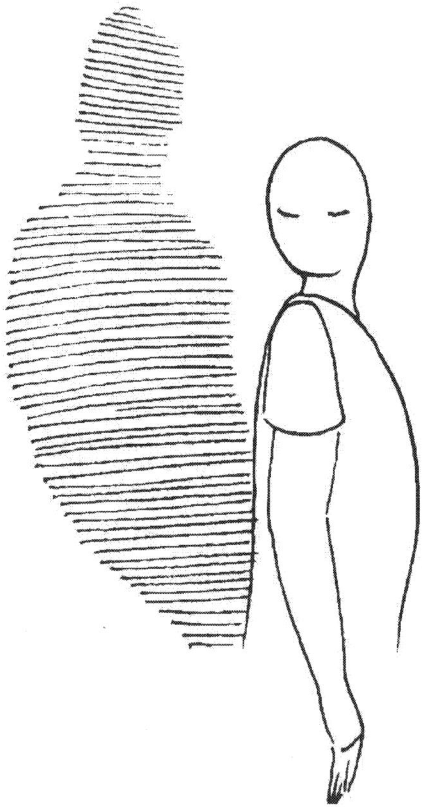

L.

I remember running
in circles on the phone
with her late one night
for hours she debated
can't remember what
I said to get out but the gist
was
it would never work out
I was heading to LA
had to give this writing
thing a real go
and she fought
and fought
to save this man
who wasn't worth
the change in her pocket
too afraid, too cowardly
to admit out loud
the truth I held
how I had
fallen in love with
another woman
behind her back
a year later
and I hadn't written
one damn word
not one
my love for you running
in circles
how could I think of anything else

back then?
and when I headed south
I left not to chase
a dream but to get away
from the coldness
of that city where
you left me,
the thought of you
being so close yet apart
from me too much
for a worthless man to bear
took me years
to write this
and I'm more
alone now
than a forgotten memory
lost in the mind
of an old drunk
and
for some reason
I don't feel so bad

About the Author

Edward Valladao lives in Inglewood, CA. He strives to tell meaningful stories regardless of form or genre. You can find his first novel, Candice Can Go, online or at various independent bookstores in the Los Angeles area. He ~~does not have social media, but~~ can be reached via email at books.ejv@gmail.com for business-related inquiries.

edwardvalladao

About the Illustrator

Mia Ohki is a Metis-Japanese-Canadian artist, born in Connecticut, USA, and raised in Alberta, Canada. She now lives and works between Edmonton and Calgary, AB. She primarily illustrates with black pen on white paper to convey her ideas, however she also uses many other visual art mediums, including sculpture and paint. She runs Mia Ohki Illustrations full time, and with her body of work growing, Mia is now working on her first exhibition.

75227156R00058

Made in the USA
San Bernardino, CA
27 April 2018